奇怪的嘎吱声

The Big Crunch

[美]威力·布莱文斯/著　[美]吉姆·帕约/绘

王婧/译

电子工业出版社·

Publishing House of Electronics Industry

北京·BEIJING

本书中文简体版专有出版权由Red Chair Press LLC通过CA-Link International LLC授予电子工业出版社，未经许可，不得以任何方式复制或抄袭本书的任何部分。

版权贸易合同登记号　图字：01-2022-0735

图书在版编目（CIP）数据

奇怪的嘎吱声 / (美) 威力·布莱文斯 (Wiley Blevins) 著；(美) 吉姆·帕约 (Jim Paillot) 绘；王婧译. -- 北京：电子工业出版社，2023.6
（胖狗和瘦狗）
ISBN 978-7-121-44941-3

Ⅰ.①奇… Ⅱ.①威… ②吉… ③王… Ⅲ.①儿童故事－图画故事－美国－现代 Ⅳ.①I712.85

中国国家版本馆CIP数据核字(2023)第077356号

责任编辑：范丽鹏
印　　刷：天津图文方嘉印刷有限公司
装　　订：天津图文方嘉印刷有限公司
出版发行：电子工业出版社
　　　　　北京市海淀区万寿路173信箱　邮编：100036
开　　本：787×1092　1/16　印张：26.25 字数：264千字
版　　次：2023年6月第1版
印　　次：2023年6月第1次印刷
定　　价：208.00元(全8册)

凡所购买电子工业出版社图书有缺损问题，请向购买书店调换。若书店售缺，请与本社发行部联系，联系及邮购电话：(010) 88254888，88258888。
质量投诉请发邮件至zlts@phei.com.cn，盗版侵权举报请发邮件至dbqq@phei.com.cn。
本书咨询联系方式：(010) 88254161 转 1862，fanlp@phei.com.cn。

目录

闪亮登场的主角们

克鲁德

艾克

绒球小姐

鲍勃

"我们为什么要跑啊？"艾克问。

"你等下就知道了。"克鲁德回答。

他们说完一溜烟儿穿过院子，然后翻过围栏，直接跳进了马丁太太的满是泥巴的花坛。

"噢，不是吧，怎么又来了啊，"克鲁德说，"这些老鼠。"

"老鼠？"艾克问，"在哪儿？在哪儿？"

"不，不是说真的老鼠。"克鲁德甩着身上的泥巴咕哝着，"太脏了，太脏了，实在是太脏了。"

"你到底在嘟囔些什么呀？"艾克问。

"你难道忘了吗？"克鲁德忍不住翻了个白眼儿，解释道，"我是在说那些坚果啊！"

"瞧，你都把我给说饿了。"艾克说。他们站了起来，一路滴答着泥点子穿过院子。这时，树林里忽然传来一阵嘈杂的嘎吱嘎吱声。

"你刚才听到了吗？"克鲁德问。

"听到什么？"艾克反问。

"就是嘎吱嘎吱的声音啊。"说着，克鲁德指了指树林，冲了过去。

艾克用了比平时快两倍的速度才追上克鲁德，"我们为什么要跑啊？"艾克问。

"吃东西的时候就会发出那种嘎吱嘎吱的声音，所以一定是有人偷了我们的食物！"克鲁德说。

"让我想一想啊，"艾克脚下一个"急刹车"停了下来，"我以为你把我们的食物全都给吃掉了呢！"

"等等，你为什么会这么想啊？"克鲁德反问。艾克指了指克鲁德的大肚皮。

"我这是为了过冬提前做准备而已。"克鲁德辩解道。

"可这会儿才六月啊！"艾克说。

3

紧接着他用两只后腿站立起来，然后模仿克鲁德的样子，摇摇晃晃地走了起来。

　　"如果你一直这样走路的话，"克鲁德说，"你的腿以后就会一直这样走下去的。"

　　"不不不。"艾克连忙四脚着地，老老实实地走起路来。

　　"咱们快走吧，"克鲁德催促道，"得赶快跟上那个声音。"

树林里的神秘幽灵 ②

　　他们沿着马丁太太的院子周围飞快地奔跑起来，越过围栏，穿过另一座院子，再绕过一个棚屋，又爬下一座小山坡，然后再穿过一片花园，最后来到了树林的边上。可艾克却突然一个"急刹车"停了下来。

“怎么了？”克鲁德问，“你不跟我一起进去吗？”

艾克使劲儿摇头，拒绝道：“树林里面太黑了，而且里面还有可怕的幽灵！”

“幽灵？”克鲁德疑惑地说，“树林里怎么会有幽灵呢，他们只会出现在地下室或者阁楼里。”

“还有破旧的狗窝里。”艾克补充道。

“没错，”克鲁德说，“还有破旧的狗窝里。”艾克紧张地大口喘着粗气。

“你不用担心，”克鲁德说，“如果真的看到幽灵的话，我会露出牙齿，还会摇晃尾巴，一定能把他给吓跑。”

“可是幽灵会吃小狗狗的。”艾克还是很害怕。

“你跟着我会很安全的。”克鲁德保证。

“你真的确定吗？”艾克不放心地问。

“哥们儿，我什么时候让你失望过呢？”克鲁德反问。艾克摇了摇头，然后战战兢兢地将一只脚踏进树林里。他一边走一边不忘叫唤两声给自己壮壮胆：“嗷……嗷！”

“那是什么？”艾克一惊一乍地问。

　　"就是一只猫头鹰而已，"克鲁德说，"快点跟上，你这个胆小鬼。"

　　"我才不是胆小鬼呢，"艾克反驳道，"我只是……谨慎而已。"艾克说完朝树林里又蹭了两步，依旧边走边叫唤两声。突然，克鲁德一脸惊恐地睁大双眼，他朝着艾克的身后指了指，然后拔腿就跑。艾克就像有跳蚤在疯狂地咬他的尾巴似的，紧紧地跟在克鲁德身后。

　　"我就知道这招儿百试百灵。"克鲁德坏坏地小声嘟囔道。他们不停地穿梭在茂密的树林里，绕过高大的树、粗壮的树、纤细的树、还有不长叶子的树。他们跑啊跑啊，直到看到一块大石头才停了下来。

一只乌龟正躲在大石头的阴凉里休息，艾克和克鲁德上前敲了敲他的龟壳。"你好啊，乌龟！"克鲁德打了个招呼。

"这可真是一个适合在树林里奔跑的好天气啊。"艾克幽默地说。乌龟从壳里探出了脑袋，他大概是想要耸耸肩，不过身上的壳实在是太碍事儿了。

"请问，你刚才听到奇怪的嘎吱嘎吱的声音了吗？"克鲁德问。乌龟慢吞吞地点了点头。

"那你知道这声音是从哪里发出来的吗？"艾克追问。乌龟先生又点了点头，可紧接着他就把脑袋缩了回去。"我们现在该怎么办呢？"艾克问。

"我也不知道。"克鲁德说。

"没准儿他是去问他的朋友了吧。"艾克俯身凑近龟壳，异想天开地说。

9

"你还在吗？"艾克冲着乌龟叫道。

"这简直是在白费力气。"克鲁德说。

"嘿嘿，"艾克走到乌龟的面前，不放弃地继续叫着，"你还在吗？"他又敲了敲龟壳，问道："能告诉我们，你是在哪里听到的声音吗？"乌龟又将脑袋探了出来，他用鼻子指了指一棵大树，那棵树的树干上有一个巨大的树洞。

"啊哈！"克鲁德兴奋地叫道，"我就知道是这样，多谢你啦，乌龟。"

克鲁德踮着脚尖悄悄地朝着大树走了过去。艾克学着克鲁德的样子，也踮着脚尖跟在克鲁德的身后。可他笨手笨脚的，"扑通"一声！

"快起来。"克鲁德小声地催促。

"踮着脚尖走路可真是太难了，"艾克抖掉身上的叶子，抱怨道。

"我们得悄悄地靠近那个小偷。"克鲁德说。

"小偷？"艾克不太明白。

"强盗，坏蛋，总之就是那个偷走了我们所有食物的窃贼。"克鲁德说。

"啊哈！"艾克恍然大悟。

"你给我安静点。"克鲁德说。

"好的。"艾克大声地回答。

"嘘嘘嘘……"克鲁德急忙说。

"你也得嘘嘘嘘……"艾克反驳道。

"停停停。"克鲁德说。

"停什么呀?"艾克追问。克鲁德抬起爪子一把捂住了艾克的鼻子,然后张着嘴巴,不出声地问:"你……听……到……了吗?"

艾克紧张地点了点头,他尾巴上的毛全都炸了起来。克鲁德悄悄地靠近了那个树洞,然后突然把头扎进了树洞里。

　　只见一只松鼠正坐在洞底，不停地把食物塞进嘴里。松鼠听到动静抬起头来，"啊——"，他发出一声尖叫。

　　"真相大白！"克鲁德大声喊道。

　　"耶！"艾克大叫，"终于逮住这家伙啦！"

　　"我们的食物在哪儿？"克鲁德质问道。

　　松鼠打了个饱嗝儿，"抱歉。"他吱吱叫着捂住自己的嘴巴，然后指了指身旁那一小堆食物。

　　"所有的食物就只剩下这些了吗？"克鲁德不敢置信地问。松鼠瞪了克鲁德一眼，突然捡起地上的一颗坚果，朝克鲁德猛地扔去，并趁机从树洞里逃了出去。

　　砰！咻！ 克鲁德和艾克眼瞅着松鼠飞奔着冲进树林里，可紧接着就听到**"啪叽"**一声，那家伙竟然一头撞到了树上。

　　"松鼠可没有看上去那么聪明啊！"艾克说。

　　"反正他没有我们狗狗聪明。"克鲁德说，"快去拿回我们的食物吧。"

扭啊，蹭啊，卡住了！

　　克鲁德说完又把头塞进了洞里，但是身体只能悬在半空中。克鲁德扭啊蹭啊，不停地拱来拱去，可就是没办法挤进树洞里。所以他只好又扭又蹭，不停地拱来拱去，想原路返回，可是他怎么都出不来了！

"把我弄出去！"克鲁德大喊。

"你在说什么？"艾克问。

"我被卡住了！"克鲁德说。

"你想要根棍子吗？"艾克问。

"不！"克鲁德大吼，"我说我被卡住了！"

"你是不是被卡住了呀？"艾克问。克鲁德不停地蹬着两条后腿挣扎着。"嘿，哥们儿，我猜你一定是卡住了，"艾克继续说，"我来帮帮你吧。"说完，他上去一把拽住了克鲁德的尾巴。

"嗷——"克鲁德疼得大叫了起来。

"看来不怎么管用啊。"艾克嘟囔道，紧接着他上去拽住了克鲁德的右腿，不管用。然后，他又拽住了克鲁德的左腿，还是不管用。最后，他忍不住上去戳了戳克鲁德的大屁股，这可太好玩了。

"嗷——"克鲁德叫得更大声了。

"嗯，"艾克思索着，说道，"这该怎么办才好呢？要不然……"艾克突然一把抓住克鲁德的两条后腿，然后使出吃奶的力气连拉带拽，嘴里还叽里咕噜不停地嘟囔着，直到……克鲁德终于被揪了出来。

16

"多谢啦，"克鲁德一屁股坐在艾克的身上，说道，"现在你进去，然后把我们的食物都拿出来。"

　　"为什么是我啊？"艾克不明白。

　　"因为只有你才能钻进这个洞里啊。"克鲁德解释道。

　　"我才不要进去呢，"艾克拒绝说，"树里可住着幽灵呢！"

　　"幽灵？"克鲁德反问，"幽灵只住在地下室里，或者阁楼里，或者破旧的狗窝里。"

　　"还有，有洞的大树里。"艾克补充道。

　　"你现在就进去！"克鲁德大吼。

克鲁德吼完就把艾克推进了树洞里。

艾克小心翼翼地把头往洞里探了探，带着哭腔说："这里面太黑了。"

"快往里走。"克鲁德说。

"我觉得我看到幽灵了。"艾克战战兢兢地说。

"你再看仔细点，"克鲁德说，"那里面只有我们的食物。"艾克的脑袋又往洞里探了探，突然……

20

咕咚！ "你没事儿吧，哥们儿？"克鲁德担心地问。

艾克在地上打了个滚儿摔到了角落里，他立刻向四周看去，试图寻找幽灵闪着亮光的眼睛。但他看见的只有成堆的食物而已。

"嘿，克鲁德！"艾克叫道。

"我在。"克鲁德回答。

"我看到我们的食物了，可问题是……我们要怎样把这些食物弄回家去呢？"艾克问。

"嗯，"克鲁德说，"让我好好想一想啊。"

克鲁德靠着大树一屁股坐了下来，然后开始了思考。一直在树林里不停地奔跑让他根本没办法进行思考，现在坐下来休息一会儿，应该会让思考变得容易很多。

一片叶子掉落在克鲁德的身旁。一只小鸟在他头顶叽叽喳喳地叫个不停。两只毛毛虫从木桩上爬了过去。然而，克鲁德却什么办法也没想出来，因为他已经不知不觉地打起盹儿来。

　　而在树洞里的艾克呢？他也在绞尽脑汁地想办法。"有啦！"艾克开心地说，"我们为什么不就在这里，把所有的食物都吃掉呢！"这简直是再绝妙不过的好主意了，艾克立马开始往嘴里塞食物。

　　"我怎么听到嘎吱嘎吱的声音了呢？"克鲁德醒了过来。

　　"**真是**太好吃啦！"艾克开心地大叫，一刻不停地嘎吱嘎吱大吃特吃起来。

　　克鲁德把头探进洞里，急忙说："你别全都吃掉呀，也给我扔点出来呀！"

"好的，"艾克大声说，"给你一块！"说完他往外去出一大块食物。"我留两块。"艾克小声嘟囔。

"给你一块，"艾克继续大声说，"我留三块。"他小声嘟囔。

"给你一块……我留四块。"

"给你一块……我留五块。"

"给你一块……我留六块。"

就这样，所有的食物全都被他们消灭一空了。

23

"问题全都解决啦！"艾克开心地说。他打了个滚儿躺在地上，伸手胡噜了一下自己的肚皮，然后向四周看了看。树洞里什么也没有了，空空如也、一无所有。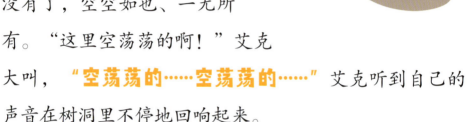"这里空荡荡的啊！"艾克大叫，**"空荡荡的……空荡荡的……"**艾克听到自己的声音在树洞里不停地回响起来。

"有幽灵啊，"艾克吓得哭喊起来，**"快点儿把我救出去啊！"**

艾克伸着胳膊不停地蹦啊蹦啊，"快点拉我上去啊，克鲁德！"艾克焦急地大叫，"我这么小可不能被幽灵吃掉啊！而且我还这么可爱更不能被幽灵吃掉啦！"

"坚持住啊，艾克！"克鲁德一把抓住艾克的两只胳膊，然后拼命地拉，使劲儿地拽，嘴里还叽里咕噜地不停嘟囔着，直到……

　　艾克终于被克鲁德从洞里揪了出来。他们翻滚着一起摔了出去，最后摔在依然昏迷不醒的松鼠身旁。"哦，糟糕……"艾克呻吟着站了起来。

　　"你不用担心那只松鼠，"克鲁德安慰他，"他今天梦里会一直梦到那些美味的坚果的。"

　　"不是，"艾克说，"我担心的不是那只松鼠，而是我的肚子。"

　　"你肚子很难受吗？"克鲁特问。

　　"非常难受。"艾克痛苦地说。

　　克鲁德戳了戳艾克的肚皮。艾克立马摇摇晃晃地站了起来。

　　"好吧好吧，"艾克说，"现在我也有个像你一样的大肚皮了，开心了吧？"

　　"我们还是回家去吧，哥们儿！"克鲁德说。

　　"好的，"艾克说，"我们回家去吧！"他们蹒跚着穿过茂密的树林，绕过高大的树、纤细的树、粗壮的树，还有不长叶子的树。

　　最后，克鲁德和艾克一起回到了他们全新的、没有幽灵的温馨狗窝。

Meet the Characters

Crud

Ick

Miss Puffy

Bob

1

Follow the Crunch

"Why are we running?" asked Ick.

"You'll see," said Crud.

They raced through their yard, jumped over the fence, and landed in Mrs. Martin's flower bed, which was still all mud.

"Oh not again," said Crud. "Rats!"

"Rats?" asked Ick. "Where?"

追踪神秘的嘎吱声 1

"我们为什么要跑啊？"艾克问。

"你等下就知道了。"克鲁德回答。

他们说完一溜烟儿穿过院子，然后翻过围栏，直接跳进了马丁太太的满是泥巴的花坛。

"噢，不是吧，怎么又来了啊，"克鲁德说，"这些老鼠。"

"老鼠？"艾克问，"在哪儿？在哪儿？"

1

“不，不是说真的老鼠。”克鲁德甩着身上的泥巴咕哝着，“太脏了，太脏了，实在是太脏了。”

“你到底在嘟囔些什么呀？”艾克问。

“你难道忘了吗？”克鲁德忍不住翻了个白眼儿，解释道，“我是在说那些坚果啊！”

“瞧，你都把我给说饿了。”艾克说。他们站了起来，一路滴答着泥点子穿过院子。这时，树林里忽然传来一阵嘈杂的嘎吱嘎吱声。

“你刚才听到了吗？”克鲁德问。

“听到什么？”艾克反问。

“就是嘎吱嘎吱的声音啊。”说着，克鲁德指了指树林，冲了过去。

2

艾克用了比平时快两倍的速度才追上克鲁德，“我们为什么要跑啊？”艾克问。

“吃东西的时候就会发出那种嘎吱嘎吱的声音，所以一定是有人偷了我们的食物！”克鲁德说。

“让我想一想啊，”艾克脚下一个“急刹车”停了下来，“我以为你把我们的食物全都给吃掉了呢！”

“等等，你为什么会这么想啊？”克鲁德反问。艾克指了指克鲁德的大肚皮。

“我这是为了过冬提前做准备而已。”克鲁德辩解道。

“可这会儿才六月啊！”艾克说。

3

“No, not rats,” said Crud, wiping off the mud. “Oh, crud, crud, crud!”

“Why are you yelling your name?” asked Ick. “Did you forget it?” Crud rolled his eyes. “I mean oh nuts,” he said.

“Now you’re making me hungry,” said Ick. The two stood up and started dripping across the yard. Just then a crunching noise drifted in from the woods.

“Did you hear that?” asked Crud.

“Hear what?” asked Ick.

“That crunching sound,” said Crud. He pointed to the woods and then took off.

Ick ran double time to keep up with him. “Why are we running?” asked Ick.

“That crunching sound is our food. Someone is stealing it.”

"Hold the doggie door," said Ick. He skidded to a stop. "I thought you were eating all our food."

"And why would you think that?" asked Crud. Ick pointed to Crud's big belly.

"I'm storing up for winter," said Crud.

"But it's only June," said Ick.

He stood on his hind legs and waddled like Crud.

"If you keep walking like that," said Crud, "your legs will freeze that way."

"Nuh-uh," said Ick. Then he dropped down on all four paws. Just in case.

"Let's keep going," said Crud. "And follow that crunch!"

紧接着他用两只后腿站立起来，然后模仿克鲁德的样子，摇摇晃晃地走了起来。

"如果你一直这样走路的话，"克鲁德说，"你的腿以后就会一直这样走下去的。"

"不不不。"艾克连忙四脚着地，老老实实地走起路来。

"咱们快走吧，"克鲁德催促道，"得赶快跟上那个声音。"

Ghost in the Trees

The two raced to the edge of Mrs. Martin's yard, over another fence, through another yard, around a shed, then down a hill, and across a small garden. But when they got to the edge of the woods, Ick skidded to a stop.

树林里的神秘幽灵

他们沿着马丁太太的院子周围飞快地奔跑起来，越过围栏，穿过另一座院子，再绕过一个棚屋，又爬下一座小山坡，然后再穿过一片花园，最后来到了树林的边上。可艾克却突然一个"急刹车"停了下来。

5

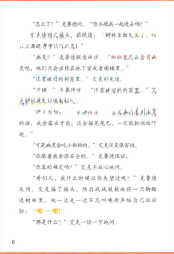

"What's wrong?" asked Crud. "Aren't you coming?"

Ick shook his head. "It's dark in the woods. And there are ghosts."

"Ghosts?" asked Crud. "Ghosts don't live in the woods. They live in basements and attics."

"And old doghouses," said Ick.

"Yes," said Crud. "And old doghouses." Ick gulped.

"Come on," said Crud. "If I see a ghost, I'll grit my teeth and shake my tail and scare it away."

"But ghosts eat little dogs," said Ick.

"You're safe with me," said Crud.

"Are you sure?" asked Ick.

"Have I ever let you down, buddy?" asked Crud. Ick shook his head. Then he put one foot inside the woods. *Hoo... hoo... hoot.*

"What's that?" asked Ick.

8

"就是一只猫头鹰而已。"克鲁德说，"快点跟上，你这个胆小鬼。"

"我才不是胆小鬼呢，"艾克反驳道，"我只是……谨慎而已。"艾克说完朝树林里又蹭了两步，依旧边走边叫唤两声。突然，克鲁德一脸惊恐地睁大双眼，他朝着艾克的身后指了指，然后拔腿就跑。艾克就像有跳蚤在疯狂地咬他的尾巴似的，紧紧地跟在克鲁德身后。

"我就知道这招儿百试百灵。"克鲁德坏坏地小声嘟囔道。他们不停地穿梭在茂密的树林里，绕过高大的树、粗壮的树、纤细的树、还有不长叶子的树。他们跑啊跑啊，直到看到一块大石头才停了下来。

一只乌龟正躲在大石头的阴凉里休息，艾克和克鲁德上前敲了敲他的龟壳。"你好呀，乌龟！"克鲁德打了个招呼。

"这可真是一个适合在树林里奔跑的好天气啊。"艾克幽默地说。乌龟从壳里探出了脑袋，他大概是想要耸耸肩，不过身上的壳实在是太碍事儿了。

"请问，你刚才听到奇怪的嗖嗖嗖的声音了吗？"克鲁德问。乌龟慢吞吞地点了点头。

"那你知道这声音是从哪里发出来的吗？"艾克追问。乌龟先生又点了点头，可紧接着他就把脑袋缩了回去。"我们现在该怎么办呢？"艾克问。

"我也不知道。"克鲁德说。

"没准儿他是去问他的朋友了吧。"艾克俯身凑过龟壳，异想天开地说。

9

"That's just an owl," said Crud. "Come on you scaredy pup."

"I'm not a scaredy pup," said Ick. "I'm just… careful." He took two more steps into the woods. Another hoot. Crud's eyes bugged out. He pointed behind Ick. And off he ran! Ick followed like a flea was chewing on his tail.

"Works every time," whispered Crud. Ick and Crud weaved in and out of the trees. Tall trees. Skinny trees. Fat trees. And trees with no leaves. They ran until they came to a big rock.

Turtle rested in the shade beside it. Ick and Crud knocked on his shell. "Hello, Turtle," said Crud.

"Nice day for a run in the woods," said Ick. Turtle poked his head out and tried to shrug, which is really hard to do in a shell.

"Did you hear a crunch?" asked Crud. Turtle slowly nodded.

"Do you know where it is?" asked Ick. Turtle nodded again, then

slid back inside his shell. "What should we do now?" asked Ick.

"I don't know," said Crud.

"Maybe he's calling a friend," said Ick. He leaned in to Turtle's shell.

"Hello?" said Ick.

"That's the wrong end," said Crud.

"Oops," said Ick. He walked to the front of Turtle. "Hello," he yelled again. Ick tapped on Turtle's shell. "Can you tell us where you heard the sound?" Turtle poked out his head. Then he pointed his nose at a large tree. It had a big hole in it.

"A-ha!" said Crud. "Just as I thought. Thanks, Turtle."

"你还在吗？"艾克冲着乌龟叫道。

"这简直是在白费力气。"克鲁德说。

"嘿嘿，"艾克走到乌龟的面前，不放弃地继续叫着，"你还在吗？"他又敲了敲龟壳，问道："能告诉我们，你是在哪里听到的声音吗？"乌龟又将脑袋探了出来，他用鼻子指了指一棵大树，那棵树的树干上有一个巨大的树洞。

"啊哈！"克鲁德兴奋地叫道，"我就知道是这样，多谢你啦，乌龟。"

Busted!

Crud tiptoed to the tree. Ick tiptoed behind him. Or tried to. *Plop.*

"Get up," whispered Crud.

"It's not easy walking on your toes," moaned Ick. He brushed off the leaves.

"We have to sneak up on that thief," said Crud.

"Thief?" asked Ick.

"Robber. Villain. The Stealer of All That Is Yummy."

"Ahh," said Ick.

克鲁德踮着脚尖悄悄地朝着大树走了过去。艾克学着克鲁德的样子，也踮着脚尖跟在克鲁德的身后。可他笨手笨脚的，"扑通"一声！

"快起来。"克鲁德小声地催促。

"踮着脚尖走路可真是太难了，"艾克抖掉身上的叶子，抱怨道。

"我们得悄悄地靠近那个小偷。"克鲁德说。

"小偷？"艾克不太明白。

"强盗，坏蛋，总之就是那个偷走了我们所有食物的家伙。"克鲁德说。

"啊哈！"艾克恍然大悟。

11

"And be quiet," said Crud.

"Got it," yelled Ick.

"*Shhh,*" said Crud.

"*Shhh* to you, too," said Ick.

"Stop it," said Crud.

"Stop what?" asked Ick. Crud put his paw on Ick's nose. He mouthed the words, "Can… you… hear… that?"

Ick nodded. The hairs on his tail stood up and curled. Crud leaned next to the hole in the tree and darted his head inside.

A squirrel sat at the bottom stuffing food into his mouth. The squirrel looked up. "Uh-oh," he squeaked.

"Gotcha!" yelled Crud.

"Yeah," yelled Ick. "Busted."

"Where's our food?" asked Crud. The squirrel burped. "Excuse me," he squeaked and covered his mouth. Then he pointed to a small pile.

"That's all that's left?" asked Crud. The squirrel just stared. Then he picked up a nut, threw it at Crud, and dashed out of the tree.

Bonk! Swoooosh! The two watched as the squirrel raced into the woods, and ran head-first into another tree. *Splat!*

"Squirrels aren't as smart as they look," said Ick.

"Not as smart as dogs," said Crud. "Let's get our food."

4

Wiggle, Squiggle, Stuck

Crud stuffed his head inside the hole, then he lifted up his body. He wiggled. And squiggled. And turned and churned. But he couldn't squeeze through. So he wiggled back. And squiggled back. And turned and churned back. But he couldn't get out.

克鲁德说完又把头塞进了洞里，但是身体只能悬在半空中。克鲁德扭啊蹭啊，不停地拱来拱去，可就是没办法挤进树洞里。所以他只好又扭又蹭，不停地拱来拱去，想原路返回，可是他怎么都出不来了！

15

"Get me out," yelled Crud.

"What?" asked Ick.

"I'm stuck," said Crud.

"You want a stick?" asked Ick.

"No," yelled Crud. "I'm stuck!"

"Are you stuck?" asked Ick. Crud kicked his legs. "Hey, I think you're stuck, buddy," said Ick. "Let me help you." Ick pulled on Crud's tail.

"*Owwwww*," yelled Crud.

"That won't work," said Ick. So he pulled on Crud's right leg. Nothing moved.Then he pulled on Crud's left leg. Nothing moved. Finally, he poked Crud's butt. But that was just for fun.

"*Owwwww*," yelled Crud again.

"Hmmm," said Ick. "What can I do? Maybe…" Ick grabbed

both of Crud's legs and he pulled and he grunted and he groaned and he tugged until out popped Crud.

"Thanks," said Crud, landing on top of Ick. "Now go in there and get our food."

"What?" asked Ick.

"Only you can fit," said Crud.

"I'm not going in there," said Ick. "Ghosts live in trees."

"Ghosts?" asked Crud. "Ghosts only live in basements and attics and old doghouses," he said.

"And big trees with holes," said Ick.

"Go!" yelled Crud.

Waddle Home

Crud pushed Ick to the hole in the tree.

Ick tipped his head inside. "It's dark in there," he cried.

"Go!" said Crud

"I think I see a ghost," said Ick.

"Look closer," said Crud. "It's just our pile of food." Ick

tipped his head further in the hole. And as he did…

蹒跚着走回家！

克鲁德吼完就把艾克推进了树洞里。

艾克小心翼翼地把头往洞里探了探，带着哭腔说："这里面太黑了。"

"快往里走。"克鲁德说。

"我觉得我看到幽灵了。"艾克战战兢兢地说。

"你再看仔细点，"克鲁德说，"那里面只有我们的食物。"艾克的脑袋又往洞里探了探，突然……

19

BAM!

Thud! "You okay, buddy?" asked Crud. Ick rolled over and scooted to the corner. He looked around for the glowing eyes of a ghost. But all he spotted was the pile of food.

"Hey Crud," said Ick.

"Yes," said Crud.

"I see our food, but… how will we get it home?"

"Hmmm," said Crud. "Let me think." Crud plopped beside the tree and began thinking. Which is hard to do after a long run in the woods. But a little easier to do when you're sitting. A leaf fell beside him. A bird chirped above him. Two worms crawled over a log. But nothing popped into Crud's head as he slowly dozed off.

而在树洞里的艾克呢？他也在绞尽脑汁地想办法。"有啦！"艾克开心地说，"我们为什么不就在这里，把所有的食物都吃掉呢！"这简直是再绝妙不过的好主意了，艾克立马开始往嘴里塞食物。

"我怎么听到嘎吱嘎吱的声音了呢？"克鲁德醒了过来。

"**真是**太好吃啦！"艾克开心地大叫，一刻不停地嘎吱嘎吱大吃特吃起来。

克鲁德把头探进洞里，急忙说："你别全都吃掉哟，也给我扔点出来哟！"

"好的，"艾克大声说，"给你一块！"说完他往外丢出一大块食物。"我留两块。"艾克小声嘟囔。

"给你一块，"艾克继续大声说，"我留三块。"他小声嘟囔。

"给你一块……我留四块。"

"给你一块……我留五块。"

"给你一块……我留六块。"

就这样，所有的食物全都被他们消灭一空了。

Inside, Ick was hard at work doing his own thinking. "I've got it!" he said. "Maybe we should eat all the food here." He popped some food into his mouth because it was such a good idea.

"I hear crunching," said Crud, as he woke up.

"It's *really* yummy," yelled Ick. He kept crunching.

Crud poked his head inside the hole. "Don't eat it all," he said. "Toss some up to me."

"Okay," said Ick. "One for you." Up flew a hunk of food. "And two for me," he whispered.

"One for you," Ick said again. "And three for me," he whispered again.

One… four…

One… five…

One… six…

And so on until all the food was gobbled up.

"We did it!" said Ick. Then he rolled on his back, grabbed his belly, and looked around. The hole in the tree now had nothing in it. Nada. Zilch. "It's empty," yelled Ick. "*Empty… Empty…*" bounced off the walls and shot back at him.

"A ghost!" cried Ick. "*GET ME OUT OF HERE!!*"

He lifted his arms and jumped up and down. "Pull, Crud," he yelled. "I'm too young to get eaten by a ghost! I'm too cute to get eaten by a ghost!"

"Hang on, Ick," said Crud. Crud grabbed Ick's arms and he pulled and he tugged and he grunted and he groaned until…

艾克终于被克鲁德从洞里揪了出来。他们翻滚着一起摔了出去，最后摔在依然昏迷不醒的松鼠身旁。"哦，糟糕……"艾克呻吟着站了起来。

"你不用担心那只松鼠，"克鲁德安慰他，"他今天梦里会一直梦到那些美味的坚果的。"

"不是，"艾克说，"我担心的不是那只松鼠，而是我的肚子。"

"你肚子很难受？"克鲁特问。

"非常难受。"艾克痛苦地说。

克鲁德戳了戳艾克的肚皮。艾克立马摇摇晃晃地站了起来。

"好吧好吧，"艾克说，"现在我也有个像你一样的大肚皮了，开心了吧？"

"我们还是回家去吧，哥们儿！"克鲁德说。

"好的，"艾克说，"我们回家去吧！"他们蹒跚着穿过茂密的树林，绕过高大的树、纤细的树、粗壮的树，还有不长叶子的树。

…out popped Ick. The two rolled away from the tree and landed beside the knocked-out squirrel. "Oh, no," moaned Ick, as he got up.

"Don't worry about that squirrel," said Crud. "He'll be dreaming about nuts for the rest of the day."

"No," said Ick. "I'm not worried about the squirrel. It's my belly."

"Your belly hurts?" asked Crud.

"Really hurts," said Ick.

Crud pointed to Ick's belly. Then Ick stood and waddled.

"Okay," said Ick. "Now it's big. Just like yours. Are you happy?"

"Let's go home, buddy," said Crud.

"Yes," said Ick. "Let's go home." And the two waddled through the woods. Tall trees. Skinny trees. Fat trees. And trees with no leaves.

最后，克鲁德和艾克一起回到了他们全新的、没有
幽灵的温馨狗窝。

28

Until they came to their doghouses. New ones.

With no ghosts.